GLOSSOP TRAM

1903-1927

by

BARRY M. MARSDEN

BA, MPhil, FSA, MIFA

1. August 21st 1903 and a laden Car 3 parked behind the loop prepares to leave the Old Glossop terminus on the inaugural run of the new tram service. No less than three public houses lay within close drinking distance of the stop, and the landlord of the 'Queen's Arms' doubtless contemplates increased profits as he poses in the doorway of his tavern. The tram conductor evidently rejoiced in the name of 'Masher' Howard. At least two versions of this interesting shot exist.

Copyright © B.M. Marsden & Foxline Publishing

ISBN   1 870119 12 6

Designed and edited by Gregory K. Fox

Typeset by Ryburn Typesetting Ltd, Halifax

Printed by Ryburn Book Production, Halifax

Published by Foxline Publishing, 32 Urwick Road,
          Romiley, Stockport SK6 3JS

Fleet Vehicles

Fleet No.	Year built/ purchased	Builders	Type	Seating	Truck	Motors	Controllers
1–7	1903	Milnes	Open-top	22/26	Milnes Girder 6'	GE58 2 x 35hp	BTH B18
8	1904	BEC	Demi-car	22	BEC 6'	Brush/ Raworth	Raworth
9	1918 (ex-Sheffield)	ERTCW	Single-deck	28	Brill 21E 7'	GE58 2 x 35hp	BTH B13

2. This original tramway junction box, in use till the 1980s, stood for some 80 years at the corner of Arundel and Surrey Streets until April 1984.

Introduction

This history is the second in a series of three which concentrate on the electric transport systems of Chesterfield, Glossop and Ilkeston. Glossop, an isolated mill town in the extreme north-west of the county, was the smallest electric tramway enterprise in Derbyshire, eventually deploying nine tramcars along a 4 mile line linking the small communities of Hadfield and Old Glossop. The private undertaking endured for only 24 years, and this little work will hopefully stand as a correct and enduring record of one small segment of a short-lived but fascinating period in the development of my native county's transport history.

Barry M. Marsden,
Eldwick 1991.

Acknowledgments

In presenting this work particular thanks are due to Ann Brown, Sue Essex and other staff of Glossop Public Library, and Peggy Davies, and her staff at Glossop Heritage Centre, who have provided willing and unstinting assistance towards the basic research. For photographs I am especially indebted to Glossop Public Library, The Glossop Heritage Centre, Jim Bennett, A.K. Kirby, the TMS and David Roberts. Other help has been kindly forthcoming from Roger Benton of the TMS and Glynn Waite. To all I would like to record my grateful appreciation.

Bibliography

Glossop Tramways

C.C. Hall Tramway
Review No 24 1958

The Tramways of
　　South East Lancashire

W.H. Bett, J.C. Gillam
Light Railway Transport
League 1976

Local History Transport Files

Glossop Library/
Heritage Centre

3. Mr Squire Sellars, who owned the High Street drapery pictured behind the tram, hired and decorated this vehicle for the opening day run. Motorman J.W. Phair, in serviceable clogs, stands alongside the car, whilst Mr Sellars' senior staff pose on the top deck.

4. An excellent postcard view of one of the brand-new cars which picks out its livery, truck details and other salient features. Note the luxury of lower saloon curtaining.

Glossop Tramways 1903–1927

The Glossop Tramway was one of three similar local systems inaugurated early in the first decade of the 20th century, that era of optimism and expansion in the history of electric traction in Britain, when new lines seemed to be opening almost every week. The three systems – Glossop, Ilkeston, and Chesterfield – all consisted of mainly single line and loop track with a route length of around four miles in each case, and an initial deployment of between six and 13 open top cars.

The Glossop and Ilkeston systems were notably similar in a number of ways. Both clung to the very edges of the county, the former in the north-west, the latter in the south-east, and both towns lay in the proximity of extensive valleys, the Longdendale and the Erewash. Both lines were barely viable propositions when first constructed, being laid in that enthusiastic heyday when hopes were high and connections with larger systems an eventual possibility. Both enterprises served fairly small populations and they were opened in just over three months of each other. There was even some similarity in the layouts, as both included a main track with a single spur line running off.

Glossop, a gritstone mill town lying in the Longdendale valley and surrounded by the High Peak, is really a child of Lancashire, though firmly established within the Derbyshire border. The choice of the small town as the site of the county's second electric tramway system (Matlock had established a cable tramway in 1893) is a surprising one. In the 1890s the Glossop Carriage Company ran a horse bus from the Norfolk Arms Hotel to the Commercial Hotel three times a day, but the vehicles were never full. Presumably the hope was that the enterprise would transport large numbers of workers who held jobs at the numerous mills and other factories along the route who would be attracted by the low fares in prospect. A further hope was that the Glossop tramway could be extended into the territory of the vast Stalybridge, Hyde, Mossley and Dukinfield Joint Board (SHMD) whose lines, covering the eastern side of Manchester and district, ran as close as Mottram, less than two tantalising miles away from Woolley Bridge, right on the county border.

It was obvious that any line laid through Glossop would have to rely on private enterprise, and the guiding spirit in this venture was Charles Edward Knowles, a local boy with a lifelong obsession in electric traction. In the winter of 1883 he had apparently exhibited the first model electric railway ever seen in the locality, at Glossop vicarage. He later served an engineering apprenticeship at the Gorton works of the Great Central Railway. He must have interested his employers, the Urban Electricity Supply Company (UESC) with the prospects offered by a joint tramway and local electricity supply company in the township, and in November 1900 the Glossop Tramways Provisional Order Bill was published, the application emanating from the UESC itself.

As shown in the original plans, the track layout was in the form of an elongated 'C' whose backbone was orientated north-west/south-east. The upper curve of the C terminated at Hadfield, the lower at Old Glossop. A spur line ran south from near the south eastern end to Charlestown. The town itself consisted of two distinct and fairly isolated parts, Hadfield and Glossop, joined by a then relatively undeveloped section of roadway following the Glossop Brook along Brookfield and Dinting Vale. Strung out along the route, and at the termination of the branch line, were a series of large mills and other works, all of which would be connected by the proposed tramline. The main track was 4 miles long on the map, though as a result of the curving route the two main termini were less than two miles apart. The branch line, usually called the Whitfield section, was a further half-mile in length.

As originally devised the tramway was planned as single track with turnouts, the line running for the most part down the centre of the streets. Nine loops were provided along the main stretch, and one on the spur line, though a tenth was added during construction to the former on Woolley Bridge Road, between the turnouts at Hadfield Road and Bank Bottom. The line incorporated a level crossing near the Pear Tree Inn on Woolley Bridge Road, whose rails transported goods along the Waterside Branch of the Great Central Railway. The tramtrack was also crossed by two bridges, one near the Spring Tavern at Brookfield, again carrying the above line, the other being the spectacular Dinting Viaduct which bore the GCR Manchester–Sheffield traffic.

The Hadfield terminus was located near the local railway station and was laid just outside the Palatine and Railway Hotel on Station

Road. The Old Glossop terminus was outside the Queen's Arms Hotel, Hall Street, and the branch line ended by the gates of Whitfield Lodge, Charlestown Road, home of Sir John Wood. The Whitfield spur was connected to the main line by a short length of double track curving west on to both lines of the 350 foot long Norfolk Square loop. Though the original plans showed the termini concluding in open-ended turnouts as at Ilkeston and Chesterfield, in the event standard loops were laid, with short stretches of single track beyond them forming the actual ends of all three stops. The gauge was set at 4' 8½" in imitation of the Manchester system with which an eventual coupling was hopefully envisaged.

Though Glossop Council had first only agreed to the main line tramway, they were persuaded by the UESC to include the Whitfield branch, and even gave permission for an extension from Hadfield to Padfield. Despite its advantages the latter scheme was scrubbed, apparently due to difficulties with a railway arch. Royal Assent was granted for the Glossop Order in 1901, with the unusual proviso that there was to be no right of municipal purchase for 57 years, dating from June 1900. By that time the line had been out of existence for some 30 years!

After the receipt of the Royal Assent, the UESC dragged its heels for some time, and only informed the Glossop Council in July 1902 that it was due to begin construction work. This was none too soon as the Order was due to expire that August if the undertaking was not commenced. A site at Dinting, on the north bank of the Glossop Brook, was selected for the tram depot and power station. The only problem was the necessity to bridge the stream to connect the shed to the main line on High Street West. Work on the power station started in August and in the autumn tracklaying commenced on the Old Glossop stretch. By December 1902 this was practically completed, the Whitfield spur line begun, and construction of the rest of the line proceeded during the winter. During that same month the Glossop Brook was bridged and the route of the single track connecting main track and tramshed was planned. Cars were to cross the bridge and emerge on to High Street West via a narrow lane between two blocks of terraced houses, which must have delighted the occupants of the end dwellings enormously! This unlikely looking depot entrance was joined to the main line by a single track junction curving east, rather than a more sensible 'Y'

arrangement. This meant a swinging of trolley poles for early morning vehicles heading towards Hadfield, and returning from thence late at night.

The rails used were the standard 92lb per yard girder type supplied by Dick, Kerr and Company, with special trackwork by Hadfields of Sheffield, and standard eight foot points. Total route length was 8,030 yards, a track length of 9,185 yards. The maximum gradient was 1 in 13 and the sharpest curve, at the Whitfield spur junction, was 38' 6" in radius. The overhead was carried mainly on bracket-arm poles which were completely functional, displaying no ornamental scrollwork whatever. Very little use was made of twin poles and span wire as all photographs of the system show.

The company ordered seven open top cars from G.F. Milnes of Hadley, all fitted with the 6 foot German girder type truck then in use by the firm. The first six cars – why not seven is not recorded – arrived by rail in July 1903, by which time all trackwork was complete. The tramshed too was finished, joined to the north side of the power station and embodying four tracks, capable of housing eight vehicles. The electric cars featured reversed staircases, offset trolleybooms and had three-windowed lower saloons which were originally furnished with curtains. The headlamps were in the dash panels, with the car number painted below, and oyster lamps on slender stands were fitted at each end of the upper deck, though their positioning seems to have varied from car to car. Each tramcar seated 26 passengers outside on ribbed wooden garden seats with reversible backs, and 22 inside on longitudinal wooden benches. Each car was 27 feet long and six feet nine inches wide over the corner pillars. Tidswell lifeguards were fitted, and hand and slipper brakes. The electrical equipment was by BTH, including GE58 35hp motors and B18 controllers. The overhead arms utilised Wood's type trolley heads, and though the upper deck had the usual safety rails, no wire mesh was ever fitted.

There is some discussion on the livery carried by the tramcars during their service in Glossop. The original colour was apparently dark green and primrose, with plain lining out on the dash panels, staircases and lower body panels only, and the legend 'GLOSSOP TRAMWAYS' was painted in gold on the rocker panel. Interestingly, all early colour postcards show the colour scheme as maroon and cream, and whilst this is never an accurate gauge to actuality, it is worthy of comment. Early black and white photographs do show the cars painted a very dark primary shade, so presumably the green was a fairly deep one. There is no information as to whether the vehicles were ever subsequently repainted in different colours.

The power station was ready for operation in August 1903. Belliss and Morcam provided the motors for the generating plant, and the dynamos were built by Parker and Company of Wolverhampton. The current was produced at 500 volts and fed to the system via underground cables running parallel to the tracks. At half-mile intervals cast iron feeder boxes, containing switches and fuses, ran the current to the overhead. The boxes also contained telephones for swift communication with the generating station. One of these boxes, at the junction of Surrey and Arundel Streets, remained *in situ* till April 1984, and though a little corroded the words 'GLOSSOP 1903 TRAMWAYS' could still be clearly seen. The whole tramway system, including the seven open toppers, cost a total of £54,000. In preparation for the opening of the line, Knowles, now Resident Engineer and Manager of the enterprise, ordered ten Bell ticket punches from Williams of Ashton-under-Lyne at a rental of 15/6d each per annum. A little later he hired an 11th punch for an extra conductor he had employed.

The first trial trip took place on Friday August 7th when a single car crossed the bridge and glided along to the first loop and back. On the evening of the 11th Car 5 ran the length of the whole line. By this time all seven vehicles were ready for service, and a formal opening was fixed for 11am on Thursday the 20th. The Board of Trade inspection was scheduled for the previous day, but was postponed to the 21st. The opening went ahead, but no services were able to commence until the BOT gave the go ahead. All the cars were decorated with flags and bunting and shown to the public on a drizzly, overcast day. Among the guests were Captain Samuel Hill-Wood, owner of the largest mill in Glossop and local benefactor, and his wife. The latter had consented to drive the leading car, which also contained the Glossop Old Band who enlivened the proceedings with a series of tuneful airs. After the ceremony the guests retired to a large marquee set up alongside the power station, and enjoyed a repast of roast beef, mutton, 'choice confectionery' and champagne,

followed by the usual complimentary and optimistic speeches. There is some dispute as to how many cars went on the trial run that day, but it appears that at least one empty open topper flew the flag on a journey to Old Glossop, leaving the depot at 11.45am then returning to Dinting via Whitfield and Hadfield. One tram had been hired for the occasion by Mr Squire Sellars who owned a large drapery business on High Street East. He filled it with his relations and staff, and it was driven at least as far as his establishment by Motorman John William Phair, as a contemporary photograph shows.

The following day the BOT examination took place and business commenced immediately. In the early days cars ran from Hadfield every 15 minutes, alternate trams going to Old Glossop and Whitfield and providing these localities with a half-hourly service. There was obviously a need to indicate which vehicles were going where, and photographs show a variety of destination boards hung over the dash panels. One stated 'Woolley Bridge Only' obviously denoting a short-working for mill personnel. Another read 'Old Glossop and Whitfield'. Some cars also had 'Hadfield' painted round the upper part of the headlamps. Presumably the customers were able to work out where their transport was headed!

The new tramway made an immediate impact on the township, carrying 3591 passengers on the first Friday, 4914 on Saturday, and 2636 on the Monday. All the original tickets purchased had sold out by the first evening, a certain Mr Robert Hamnett buying the first 12 ever issued. One 85 year old lady, bedridden but still alert, saw the crowded open toppers from her upstairs window and wailed 'Aye – all the enjoyment is starting now when the old folks have to die!' The original fare was 2d a ride for all journeys, though in the first full week of service four penny stages were introduced, from the Old Glossop terminus to Whitfield or the Junction Inn, from the latter to Woolley Bridge, from the Printworks to Hadfield Catholic Church and from Woolley Bridge to the Hadfield terminus. The through journey remained at 2d. Between 5.30 and 7am and 5.30–6.30pm workmens' fares were available with halfpenny stages, and weekly tickets were also issued; at some stage in the history of the enterprise these cost 6d.

The line had its teething troubles as the running of the service commenced very much on an *ad hoc* basis, with little apparent thought as to the best passing places. Solving these problems led to a number of delays, and it was not until the end of September that stopping places were agreed upon and signs either affixed to the poles or painted on their sides. Once these difficulties had been resolved the journey times speeded up, though no official timetable was produced until the following June. The Company contemplated carrying goods along the track from the large mills to the railway station, but abandoned the idea, although on the only other tramway they owned, the Camborne and Redruth line, they did operate a successful mineral traffic over the tramway which continued after passenger operations ceased.

The isolated little line had a very successful start. By January 1904 it had conveyed its first half million passengers at the rate of over 20,000 a week, although the Whitfield spur had proved something of a white elephant. At a 1920 inquiry into tramway charges, witnesses conceded it had been a mistake to build it. It 'practically ran empty' the quarter-hour service carrying only 3–4 persons per car. In February 1904 the branch line fare was reduced to ½d; by this time it may have been operating as a separate service. The only serious accident suffered by the system occurred on the spur line, and took place on the evening of Sunday March 20th, 1904. The car, number unknown, was being driven by James Cavanagh from the Whitfield terminus. At the Littlemoor slope the brakes failed, and the tramcar, swaying and rattling, began picking up speed as it approached the junction with High Street. The car contained a number of passengers, and the quick-thinking conductor, James Fidler, closed the door to prevent them leaping off in panic, then disengaged the trolley arm to prevent it ripping down the running wire. The tram jumped the points at High Street and careered across the road in the direction of Hepworth's tailors (now Barclay's Bank). At the last moment it veered aside and mounted the pavement outside Shoebridge's shop, the weight of the truck wheels causing the flagstones to partly collapse and expose the cellar beneath. Fortunately no one was injured, and the travellers were able to disembark, shaken but unhurt.

The first tramway timetable appeared in late June 1904, and was effective from July 1st. it read:

Old Glossop and Whitfield to Hadfield.
Mondays, Tuesdays, Wednesdays and Thursdays.

5.18, 5.35, 6.00am and every 15 minutes to 7.15, 8.8, 8.30, 8.50am and every 20 minutes to 4.50, 5.00, 5.18, 5.36, 5.54, 6.00, 6.12, 6.30, 6.50, 7.10, 7.30pm and every 20 minutes to 10.30pm.

Fridays: as above to 6.50am then 7.00. 7.15am and every 15 minutes to 10.45pm.

Saturdays: as above until 12.00 mid-day then 12.15pm and every 15 minutes to 11.00pm.

Sundays: 10.00am, 12.00 mid-day, 2.00pm then every 15 minutes to 10.15pm.

Cars due at Town Hall – five minutes later than above.
At Junction Inn – ten minutes later.
At Plough Inn – 15 minutes later.
At Woolley Bridge – 20 minutes later.

Hadfield to Old Glossop.
Mondays, Tuesdays, Wednesdays and Thursdays.

5.18, 5.40, 6.00am and every 15 minutes to 7.15, 8.00, 8.20, 8.35, 9.00am and every 20 minutes to 5.00, 5.18, 5.40, 5.54, 6.12, 6.30, 6.50, 7.00pm and every 20 minutes to 10.40pm.

Fridays: as above until 7.00pm then every 15 minutes to 10.45pm.

Saturdays: as above until 12.00 noon then every 15 minutes to 11.00pm.

Sundays: 10.00am, 12 noon, 2.00pm then every 15 minutes to 10.15pm.

Cars due at Woolley Bridge – 8 minutes later than above.
At Plough Inn – 15 minutes later.
At Junction Inn – 17 minutes later.
At Town Hall – 22 minutes later.

The timetable shows that a return trip over the 4 mile main line took an hour with standing time. This included a mandatory halt at Glossop Town Hall to allow for Whitfield passengers meeting the connection for cars going in either direction along the main line. The 15 minute service required four trams and the 11 minute service all vehicles, allowing for one on the Whitfield spur. The most unusual feature of the timing was the 53 minute gap (7.15–8.08am) on the Old Glossop–Hadfield run, and the ¾ hour gap at around the same time for cars going the other way.

Halfpenny stages were introduced later in July, though these did not answer local demands for a ½d fare from Old Glossop to the Town Hall. There were eight halfpenny stages, as follows:

Old Glossop	–	Sheffield Road
Sheffield Road	–	Town Hall
Whitfield	–	Town Hall
Town Hall	–	Junction Inn
Junction Inn	–	Shaw Lane
Shaw Lane	–	Woolley Bridge
Woolley Bridge	–	Bank Bottom
Bank Bottom	–	Hadfield

1½d stages also came in at the same time, and included the journeys between:

Old Glossop/Whitfield	–	Shaw Lane
Town Hall	–	Woolley Bridge
Junction Inn	–	Bank Bottom
Shaw Lane	–	Hadfield

At last the undertaking had a regularised and viable schedule of operations.

In August 1904 a new vehicle appeared, obviously destined to take over the Whitfield route. The single-deck tram, a demi-car, was one of only a few of this type operating in the United Kingdom, and was built by the British Electric Car Company at Trafford Park. The tram was a completely enclosed boxy-looking vehicle with a slightly rounded dash panel and front windows, and a four-light clerestory roof. It had a headlamp in the lower dash and the number 8 above. Access was by open door panels in the vestibules. The rear rocker panels carried the legend 'Passengers enter by the driver's platform.' Each vestibule featured three frontal drop windows, and one on each side, and the saloon had two windows to each side. 16 passengers could be seated longitudinally in the saloon, and three in each vestibule, a total of 22. The little car, which had a 6 foot wheelbase BEC truck, utilised Raworth regenerative equipment, comprising controllers and two Brush-Raworth shunt wound motors. This equipment stored current on downhill runs to help boost the car up gradients. On this route the conductor was dispensed with and the motorman collected the fares. It must have been a popular car to man in winter, having full driver protection. The hallmark of the Glossop motorman must have been the ruddy and weatherbeaten countenances typical of their breed, and this was the only car used which offered shelter from the elements. Doubtless this was a sought-after boon, as driving and riding in open toppers in the foothills of the winter Pennines provided ideal conditions for the onset of hypothermia!

The Glossop line was one of the smallest in Britain, comparable to Ilkeston, Wrexham and Kidderminster, and larger only than the mini-service at Taunton. The population served was only 22,000 and weekly receipts worked out at £100–135, an average of 8d per car mile. In June 1905 the timetable was revised to provide a uniform service over all five weekdays. The actual times of all trams were specified, with the first car leaving Old Glossop at 5.10am. The revamped service ran as follows:

Old Glossop–Hadfield:

5.10 5.18 5.35 6.00 6.15 6.30 6.45 7.00 7.15 8.08 8.30 9.50
10.10 10.30 10.50 11.00 11.30 11.50 12.10 12.30 12.50 1.10
1.30 1.50 2.10 2.30 2.45 3.00 3.15 3.30 3.45 4.00 4.15 4.30
4.45 5.00 5.18 5.36 6.00 6.12 6.30 6.45 7.00 7.15 7.30 7.45
8.00 8.15 8.30 8.45 9.00 9.15 9.30 9.50 10.10 10.30

On Friday nights after 9.30, cars ran at 9.45, 10.00, 10.15, 10.30 and 10.45pm.

On Saturdays there was a 15 minute service from 11.30am–2.00pm, then every 10 minutes up to 11pm. The Whitfield car left for Hadfield and Old Glossop the same time after 5.10am. Sunday services remained as before, and special cars ran every night for Hadfield, after performances at the local theatre. There remained a gaping 53 minute 'hole' between 7.15–8.08am.

Hadfield–Old Glossop:

5.18 5.40 6.00 6.15 6.30 6.45 7.00 7.15 8.00 8.20 8.35 9.00 9.20 9.40 10.00 10.20 10.40 11.00 11.20 11.40 12.00 12.20 12.40 1.00 1.20 1.40 2.00 2.20 2.40 3.00 3.15 3.30 3.45 4.00 4.15 4.30 4.45 5.00 5.18 5.40 6.00 6.12 6.30 6.45 7.00 7.15 7.30 7.45 8.00 8.15 8.30 8.45 9.00 9.15 9.30 9.40 10.00 10.20 10.40

On Fridays after 9.30pm cars ran at 9.45, 10.00, 10.15, 10.30 and 10.45. On Saturdays they operated a 15 minute service between 12 and 2.00pm, then every 10 minutes till 11pm. Sunday services again remained unchanged. The rather long morning gap after 7.15am remained unchanged.

Research into the history of the system is handicapped by the fact that it was a private company concern, and not the responsibility of the local council. Hence there are no tramway committee minutes to provide information on the running of the enterprise, and as the line was only one of a number of UESC responsibilities, it is difficult to isolate statistics and measure the prosperity of the undertaking. Before the First World War it is clear that the tramway barely met its costs, a factor not helped by a depression in the cotton trade in 1910, which lowered receipts considerably, a circumstance made worse by a heavy outlay on repairs to the track. Repairs of course came from the general UESC fund, which provided the revenue required for upkeep.

John William Phair, from Padfield, was one of the original motormen; he first drove trams in Blackpool, joining the Company after service in the Boer War. Apparently the car crews needed other skills. He helped fix the original tram standards and running wire, and also assisted with repairs. He described a severe frost one winter which actually froze the tram wheels to the line; the whole track length was encased in solid ice. The wheels had to be hacked free, and the service was badly disrupted. Other contemporaries recalled that the worst blackspot for car derailments was Bank Bottom at the north end of Station Road. The trams often carried unusual freight – local women sent their husbands' dinners down to the Dinting Printworks, and in slightly later times films were delivered to the cinemas at Glossop and Woolley Bridge. Lord Doverdale was apparently a regular passenger on the Whitfield branch, and others recollect children using the rails for the game of 'bull and hook', attempting to run for considerable distances whilst keeping a metal hoop revolving in the grooves.

In those pre-war years the directors of the UESC line received encouragement on several occasions to think that Glossop was to be connected to the bigger tram networks to the west. The SHMD turned down the idea as early as October 1903, but hopes were boosted in subsequent years. The East Cheshire Light Railways mooted a scheme in 1903–4 which was successfully opposed by the Great Central Railway, and in 1908 and 1910 two further promoters unsuccessfully put forward plans to link Glossop to larger complexes. The last attempted linkup was projected in 1915 when the SHMD gained Royal Assent for an Act which included two lines to Woolley Bridge via Stalybridge and Hyde, both channelled through Mottram. In each case the proposed lines were less than two miles long, but the ambitious and doubtless viable scheme was killed off by the war.

At some time between 1905 and 1909 the halfpenny stage must have been suspended, as in February of the latter year Knowles announced the reintroduction of the fare from March 1st 1909. The reduction was restored 'with a view to improving the revenue and to meet the wishes of the travelling public'. The change was 'to be considered in the nature of an experiment for a few months only, until it is seen whether the public take advantage of the reduced fares in sufficient numbers to warrant a permanent arrangement'. At the same time workmens' travelling time was extended to 8.15 am 'to meet the convenience of schoolteachers and shop assistants'

continued on page 12

5. Glossop Tramways Staff 1903. Motormen and conductors parade in smart 'maternity jacket' rig in front of one of the new cars outside the Dinting tramshed. Superintendent Emmett takes the controls, and on his left is Charles Knowles the General Manager. The photograph provides excellent close detail of the vehicle. A majority of the staff display fashionable hirsute adornment, whilst the Superintendent sports a full set!

though workmens' reduced lunchtime fares were abolished (except on Saturdays) and workmens' return tickets were introduced, to be available on the day of issue only.

By 1912 the Glossop line was moving towards more prosperous times, and there was a need to increase the rolling stock. Throughout the 'teens the undertaking maintained a service of 5.9 cars throughout the 16 hour day, and presuming an increase in rush-hour loads and the need for vehicle overhaul, the purchase of an extra tram was obviously felt necessary. In March 1913 Knowles enquired if Sheffield had any two-deck single truck cars for disposal. He received a negative answer, followed by a further one when he checked on the availability of any single-deckers. An advertisement in the technical press for a small double-decker with GE58 motors and B18 controllers was likewise unsuccessful. It was not until 1918 that the undertaking was able to augment its fleet. In August 1917 Knowles advertised for either one or two new or second-hand trailer tramcars or a double-deck single truck car of around 58 seat capacity with GE58 motors and B18 controllers.

Sheffield Corporation had at the time some surplus single-deckers for disposal, and these were offered to Glossop at £350 each, or £150 without equipment. In September 1917 the manager inspected the sale vehicles at the Queen's Road works. He chose car 56, built by the Electric Railway and Tramway Carriage Works, Preston in 1899 and in service in the city by 1900. The eight ton car, which boasted five side windows, a clerestory roof and roof-mounted headlamps, was mounted on a 7 foot Brill 21E truck and had been extensively overhauled in 1904 when it received a dwarf trolley base, transverse garden seats and Magrini type drop windows to improve ventilation. The vehicle, which lacked driver protection, was an obvious choice, though Knowles also tried to interest his directors in buying a second offering as well, Brush-bodied No 96, mounted on a 6 foot wheelbase truck. They demurred, and he was only able to conclude negotiations for the ERTCW built tram.

The 28 seater left Sheffield for Glossop by rail on February 13th 1918, though it reached its destination slightly damaged, the under-window beading on one side having been smashed. As the UESC intended to run the car in its Sheffield livery, they claimed the costs of repainting in the repairs. The single-decker took its first journey on the 18th March in the dark blue and cream of its original owners, though it is not known whether the Glossop Tramways logo was painted on the rocker panel. Presumably the No 56 was painted out and 9 substituted, though there is no confirmatory evidence for this.

Full particulars are available for the running of the line between 1913–20, and these show a general rise both in passengers and costs. Between 1913–16 fare stages are recorded as ½d, 1d, 1½d and 2d. In 1917 a 3d stage was introduced, and the ½d fare was phased out in 1918, a short-lived 2½d stage being added. By 1919 the fares were 1d, 1½d, 2d and 3d, but by 1920 the full fare had risen to 4d, a 100% increase on the 1913 position. It is clear that the tramway never made enough profit to meet the provision required for upkeep, leaving nothing for interest charges or return on capital. In all its working life it never earned more than 3½% gross on the balance of capital invested, and no dividend had been paid in the ten years before 1920. Fortunately the UESC, with £1 million capital, had a general depreciation fund for the whole company, which allowed them to subsidise the shortfall.

In the years 1913–19 the balance between revenue and expenditure was never very high. The best year was 1919 when profits reached £2154, but in 1914 it was as low as £580. Total expenditure rose from £5800 in 1914 to £9756 in 1919, and the amount required for upkeep doubled from £2000 to £4000 in the same period. Total revenue went up from £6828 in 1913 to £11910 in 1919, but repairs rose from £1775 to £2278, and power costs from £1690 to £2038. Car mileage dwindled at the same time – from 210,000 miles in 1913 to 196,000 in 1917. It fell to 189,000 in 1918, and again to 161,700 in 1920 when the full effects of the closing of the Whitfield branch were felt. Receipts per car mile escalated from 7.78d in 1913 to 17.07d six years later. During the same period expenditure climbed from 6.84d to 13.98d! Passenger numbers likewise fluctuated, rising to a record 1,905,501 in 1916, but falling away to 1,778,441 three years later.

The Glossop service undoubtedly suffered from shortages and rising costs during the war. By 1918 fares had risen and cars ceased to run at 10.00pm every night. That March cuts were forced on the car and repair crews; the former worked a 63 hour week, the latter 53. On the 20th of the month these hours were reduced to 48 and 47

continued on page 14

6. Glossop Tramways Staff. In this shot the tramways staff show off a different rig, perhaps an alternative summer uniform. Two inspectors flank the nattily dressed and unidentified gentleman in the centre of the photograph.

respectively. The Board of Trade called on tramways to reduce their mileage by 15% to save on coal, and the UESC responded by closing down the Whitfield spur that autumn. It was never reopened though the tracks and overhead remained *in situ*. The council turned a blind eye to these penalty-incurring actions on the part of the company. On June 30th 1919 the cotton mills altered their working hours, commencing at 7.45am. Workmens' tickets were subsequently issued between 5.45 and 8.00am to cope with the change.

In June 1920 the UESC offered to sell the tramway to the Glossop Town Council, and a sub-committee was set up to consider the proposal. They decided the asking price was too high, and called in a consultant who assisted them in determining an acceptable sum. However when the matter was placed before the full council the majority were opposed to it, and the idea was dropped. By this time the whole enterprise was in a poor state. The track condition was bad, with heavily worn rails which needed renewal within five years. The rail joints were badly dished, and the 'Dicker' fishplates required extensive welding. All the points were likewise worn and needed replacement. Increasing motor traffic had damaged the concrete foundations and the granite setts were in need of renewal, as were the trolley wires, which were badly worn. The bracket arms of the tram poles were heavily eroded by 'the corrosive nature of the Glossop atmosphere' and the clips and collars were likewise in poor condition. The original tramcars were reported to be 'badly deteriorating' and needed replacing within five years. Total renewal, including four new cars at £1500 each, would cost in the neighbourhood of £48,000. The whole picture was familiar enough in the early postwar period – a neglected and ageing system in dire need of an injection of capital. Little wonder that the UESC wished to rid themselves of a millstone of increasing weight.

By 1920 the National and District Joint Industrial Councils for the tramway industry (the 'Whitley Scheme') had been set up nationwide. In May of that year the tramway trade unions on the Councils demanded a pay rise of 10s a week. After discussion the National Council recommended a 6s rise, but in view of the parlous financial state of some undertakings, added a proviso that any system could appeal for exemption from the extra payment. Glossop Tramways' appeal was allowed but the staff not unnaturally refused to accept this, and gave a week's notice to strike. To alleviate their increasing problems the UESC had applied to the Ministry of Transport under the 1920 Tramways Act to raise fares. This had been agreed and doubtless the Glossop staff felt they should glean some benefit from the increases. Under the new scales the company charged 2d per mile, or part of a mile, for any journey. The old 2d fare went up to 3d, and the full through fare rose to 4d. They also decided to arbitrarily restrict workmens' tickets to between 5.45 and 7.00am.

On June 26th, in view of the increased journey costs, the UESC offered the Glossop staff a 6s per week rise, plus a farthing an hour on the basic wage rate. The employees rejected this claiming retrospective arrears from April, and ½d an hour basic increase. Following the deadlock, the tramways staff, against the advice of their leaders, came out on strike for ten days. The strikers produced what Knowles called 'a grossly misleading and libellous pamphlet' on their position – sadly no copies of this document seem to have survived.

continued on page 16

7. The Hadfield terminus was situated in front of the Palatine and Railway Hotel opposite the railway station. Car and crew pose on the loop, with Station Road on the left.

BUS TERMINUS. HADFIELD.

8. This view from the junction of Railway Street and Station Road shows Hadfield in the mid to late 1920s following introduction of bus services by the North Western Road Car Company. The postcard from which the view is reproduced was one of a series marketed by Messrs Lilywhite Ltd., of Triangle, Halifax, and sold locally by J.H. Bradshaw, 126 Station Road, Hadfield. At this point, the tram route was double track, the bus on this occasion rather inconveniently occupying the 'down' line. The building to the left is the library. *Photo: courtesy A.K. Kirby*

The contemporary local press is a good indicator of public attitudes to the dispute. A letter in the *Glossop Chronicle* of July 2nd felt that the pay of a motorman (£2.19) and a conductor (£2.12) was grossly deficient. Knowles however quoted average mid-1920 wages as £3.8.3d and £3.3.3d respectively, as against pre-war weekly rates of £1.7.6d and £1. The writer did think however, in view of general pay rises since the war, that 4d for the through tram journey was a fair price to ask. In the next issue *Pro Bono Publico* described the fares as 'extortionate' and the new system of workmens' tickets as 'sheer humbug and bluff, and an insult to the intelligence of the inhabitants of the district.' Another scribe also condemned the latter, complaining that it was 'compelling them to go to their work in some cases one hour before they need, or else pay double excess fare.' A third writer felt 'these cars must run at the time convenient for the great mass of the workpeople.' The newspaper itself criticised the timing of the workpeoples' tickets, whilst supporting the necessity of increased fares.

After ten days the Glossop staff returned to work on the original terms proposed by the UESC. Knowles felt the strike had been a complete failure. 'The men were badly led' he wrote 'or as some say driven by hot-heads whom they have to thank for ten days' holiday without pay.' With the rise in through fares to 4d, there was a 14% increase in takings, but a 20% decrease in public use. During the 11 weeks following the increase 53,000 workmen and 264,000 ordinary passengers were carried on the tramway, which at this time ran its first cars at 6.30am. In September there was an inquiry into the UESC decision to push fares up, due to objections by various local bodies.

The main objectors were Glossop Town Council and the Glossop and Hadfield Trades and Labour Council (GHTLC). Both bodies felt the increase to be exorbitant; the former wanted overlapping quarter-mile fare stages, workmens' fares available up to 8.00am and after 5.30pm, and the reopening of the Whitfield branch. The GHTLC wanted a rate of 1d a mile up to a maximum of 4½d and return workmens' fares at the single rate up till 8.30am. Glossop Council were prepared to accept the fare increase if workmens' fare periods were adjusted to their proposal. Eventually fares were standardised at the maximum rate of 4d, and the Whitfield spur remained closed. It must be assumed that the little

22 seat BEC demi-car was transferred to the main line after 1918, and continued to run till the end of the service.

By 1923, when hopes of a connecting line with the SHMD had long since faded, the Joint Board obtained an Act which gave it powers to run motorbuses along the proposed tramway routes authorised by its 1915 Act. Thus was the town opened to the great western networks; in fact the first Glossop motor omnibus ran three years later, in 1926. The trams continued to operate, the ride becoming bumpier and the track and equipment steadily more decrepit. Between 1923 and 1925 it still transported around a million passengers per annum, and in the latter year the cars still managed 180,000 route miles, though revenue fell from £10,500 to £9,700. In 1926 170,000 miles were run, earning receipts of £7,300. During the final year of operation car mileage slightly increased, though revenues dropped to just under £7,200 and the percentage of working costs to passenger payments was a lofty 118.3%.

In November 1927 the UESC applied to the Ministry of Transport to prolong the charges authorised by the 1920 Act, but it is now clear that they had made the decision to relinquish their control of the undertaking. They made an offer to Glossop Council, indicating their willingness to transfer the operation into municipal ownership if the former would use the company power supply. The offer was refused, and the company announced that the tramway would close down on Christmas Eve. In the event, the last trams left the Old Glossop and Hadfield termini at 11.00pm on December 24th, rattling their way into oblivion. Thirty employees received severance pay of £5 – a fine Christmas present! – and were then out of work. The local press commented:

'So we are tramless, the well-upholstered vehicles having been withdrawn on Christmas Eve. We are told they did not pay; there was not much about them to attract would-be passengers. The fares were disproportionate and the cars were uncomfortable. It is a moot question whether until they are linked up with some other system, they will ever pay. Glossop leads nowhere and the population is limited'.

The district was not long without transport as on Boxing Day the North Western company commenced an omnibus service

continued on page 20

59132   Station Road, Hadfield.   J.V.

9. A short distance down Station Road Car 1 climbs the cobbled thoroughfare towards the terminus, passing Salisbury Street on the left. Note the plain and unadorned tram standards, and the offset trolleypole on the tram, which had 'HADFIELD' painted round the dashlamp. The usual urchins and other bystanders add animation to the scene.

GLOSSOP TRAMWAYS.

REVISION of TIME-TABLE.

CARS LEAVE OLD GLOSSOP FOR HADFIELD.

Week Days.

5 10	5 18	5 35	6 0	6 15	6 30
6 45	7 0	7 15	8 8	8 30	9 50
10 10	10 30	10 50	11 10	11 30	11 50
12 10	12 30	12 50	1 10	1 30	1 50
2 10	2 30	2 45	3 0	3 15	3 30
3 45	4 0	4 15	4 30	4 45	5 0
5 18	5 36	6 0	6 12	6 20	6 45
7 0	7 15	7 30	7 45	8 0	8 15
8 30	8 45	9 0	9 15	9 30	9 50
10 10	10 30				

Friday night after 9 30 p.m., then 9 45, 10 0, 10 15, 10 30, and 10 45.

Saturdays from 11-30 a.m. every fifteen minutes up to 2 p.m., then every ten minutes up to 11 p.m.

Whitfield Car leaves for Hadfield and Old Glossop same time after 5 10 a.m.

Sundays:—10 0, 12 0, 2 0, then every 15 minutes up to 10 15.

Cars are due at the Town Hall 5 minutes later than above, at Junction Inn 10 minutes later, at Plough Inn 15 minutes later, at Woolley Bridge 20 minutes later.

THEATRE CARS.

Special Cars are run every night at end of Performance for Hadfield.

CARS LEAVE HADFIELD FOR OLD GLOSSOP AND WHITFIELD.

Week Days.

5 18	5 40	6 0	6 15	6 30	6 45
7 0	7 15	8 0	8 20	8 35	9 0
9 20	9 40	10 0	10 20	10 40	11 0
11 20	11 40	12 0	12 20	12 40	1 0
1 20	1 40	2 0	2 20	2 40	3 0
3 15	3 30	3 45	4 0	4 15	4 30
4 45	5 0	5 18	5 40	6 0	6 12
6 30	6 45	7 0	7 15	7 30	7 45
8 0	8 15	8 30	8 45	9 0	9 15
9 30	9 40	10 0	10 20	10 40	

Fridays after 9 30 a.m., then 9 45, 10 0, 10 15, 10 30, 10 45.

Saturdays from 12 to 2 every fifteen minutes, then every 10 minutes up to 11 o'clock.

Sundays:—10 0, 12 0, 2 0, then every fifteen minutes up to 10 15.

Cars are due at Woolley Bridge 8 minutes later than above, at Plough Inn 15 minutes later, at Junction Inn 18 minutes later, at Town Hall 22 minutes later.

GLOSSOP ELECTRIC TRAMWAYS.

IMPORTANT NOTICE.

With a view to improving the revenue, and to meet the wishes of the travelling public, I have pleasure in announcing that my directors have sanctioned the

RE-INTRODUCTION OF HALFPENNY FARES ON MARCH 1st.

This change is, however, to be considered in the nature of an experiment for a few months only, until it is seen whether the public take advantage of the reduced fares in sufficient numbers to warrant a permanent arrangement.

Workmen's Travelling Time in Morning will be Extended to 8-15 a.m.,

To meet the Convenience of School Teachers and Shop Assistants. Workmen's Reduced Fares during dinner hour (except on Saturdays) will be abolished.

WORKMEN'S RETURN TICKETS, available on day of issue only, will be introduced; the return half being available on any car during the day.

URBAN ELECTRIC SUPPLY COMPANY, Ltd.,
C. E. KNOWLES, Resident Engineer and Manager.

◁ **10. Opposite** At exactly the same spot as plate 9, but travelling uphill, a near empty Car 2, again with 'HADFIELD' painted round the lamp, poses for the camera on the incline near Roberts' Music Stores.

11. A good view of the steep descent faced by passengers headed towards Glossop, with Wesley Street on the left, below the Post Office. The photograph clearly shows the stone setts extending on both sides of the single line, and whose upkeep was the responsibility of the tramway company.

along the abandoned route. For some time after the closure the locals felt the departure of the trams was only temporary, and as late as March 1928 the council were still debating a take-over. By April however the UESC had agreed to remove the rails and reinstate the roadway. A 24 year episode was finally closed; parodying *King Lear*, one might comment 'The wonder is it hath endured so long'. The fate of the tramcars is unknown; presumably they were stripped and sold off locally, sharing the destiny of those in Chesterfield, Ilkeston and elsewhere.

Perhaps the shades of Charles Knowles and others might smile wryly and ironically at the recent proposals by the Greater Manchester PTE for the introduction of a 'supertram' network across the city in the 1990s. In July 1989 the *Daily Telegraph* reported that 'The PTE is already looking ahead to its extension along six major radials, including Glossop'. Maybe the last decade of this troubled century might see an LRT link from the isolated township via Woolley Bridge along a new tramway network to the west, finally realising the great dreams of the electric transport planners of pre-World War 1.

12. Car 3, well-laden with young ladies perhaps on an outing, descends Station Road above Lambgates in the early years of the service. The board hung on the dash panel indicates that the vehicle serves both the main line and the Whitfield spur.

13. A well-known shot, showing a fully-patronised and worse-for-wear Car 3, conveying a cargo of cloth-capped workmen on a short haul to Woolley Bridge. The tram is pictured on Woolley Bridge Road near the junction with Bank Bottom.

14. At the east end of Woolley Bridge Road the line, here offset to the side of the thoroughfare, took trams past John Walton's mill complex.

15. BEC demi-car No 8, photographed on delivery, with Charles Knowles on the driver's platform. The lines of the boxy little single-decker, with its prominent clerestory roof, show up well.

16. In 1918 the tramway took delivery of a single-deck ex-Sheffield car, No 56, here seen in earlier service in the city. The 'SV' sign indicated its usual route as 'Spring Vale.' The UESC ran the tram in its Sheffield livery.

17. The tramtrack ran through rural scenery at Brookfield, here shown with Brookfield Mill in the distance, and Shaw Lane on the right. This shot captures the first appearance of a motorbus in the town in 1926 when the SHMD exercised its rights to run omnibuses under its 1915 powers. The nearest tram standard has a 'STOP' sign painted on it. A caravan sales park now occupies the open ground to the left of the vehicle. To the left of the bus is the outline of the bridge carrying the GCR Waterside Branch.

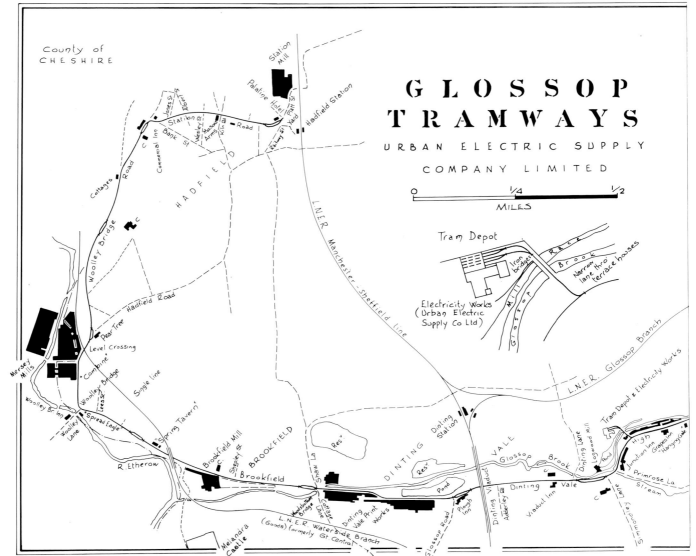

continued opposite

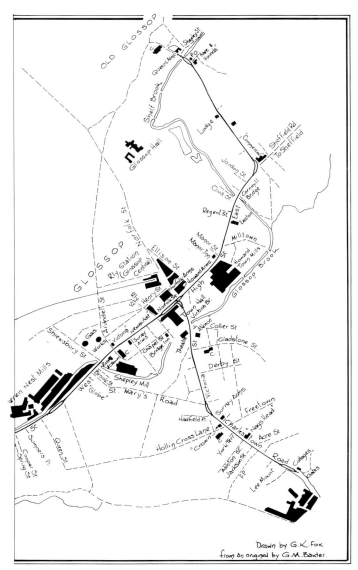

18. Fortunately, the postcard view reproduced here was safely kept by Mr B. Lee of Godley, Hyde. It shows his mother, Mrs Alice Lee, in her conductress' uniform of Glossop Tramways – note the UESC badge on the right lapel – in 1916. Mrs Lee came to Glossop from Sheffield, age 10, in 1905 as Alice Whitworth. In 1915 she married Henry Lee, a Glossop tram driver, who at the time of the photograph was serving abroad with the armed forces.

Photo: courtesy Mr B. Lee

continued opposite

19. This view along Dinting Vale towards Glossop shows a scene and location which has changed little over the years. The spire of Holy Trinity Church continues to dominate whilst the cottages to the right survive, externally at least, in their original form.

Photo: courtesy A.K. Kirby

20. The spectacular Dinting Viaduct dominated the view as the line passed through the open Dinting Vale. In this photograph, looking north-west, Holy Trinity Church is on the right and beyond the arch on the left was the Plough Inn, halfway stage on the main route.

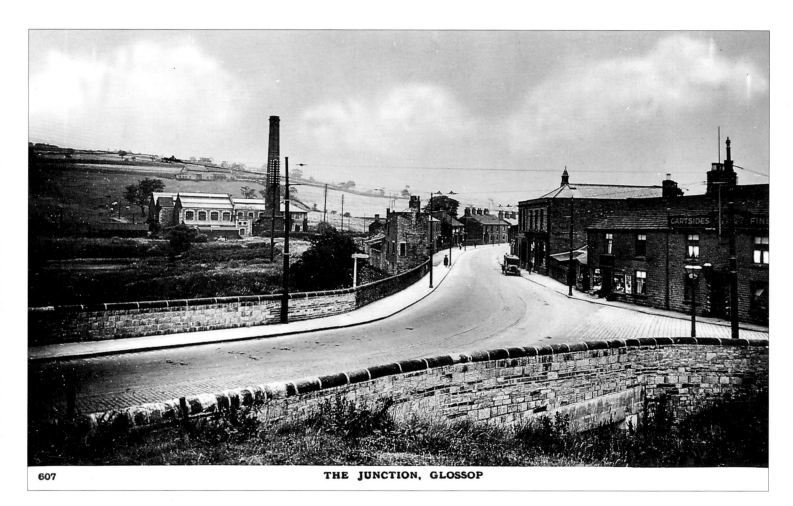

607   **THE JUNCTION, GLOSSOP**

21. The bottom of Simmondley Lane provided the vantage point for this view of the junction where Primrose Lane and Dinting Vale met High Street West. The Junction Inn is to the right. Of particular interest however are the buildings on the middle ground, to the left of the picture, which housed the generating equipment of the Urban Electricity Supply Company, owners and operators of Glossop Tramways. The tram shed was to the rear, abutting the Electricity Works.   *Photo: Barrett & Co, courtesy A.K. Kirby*

22. The unimposing central gap between this terrace on High Street West, behind the photographer's youthful audience, was the entrance to the tram depot which was reached via a bridge over the Glossop Brook. Swann's fine clock shows the time as 12.16pm, an unselfconscious dog is caught in the act, and the scattered deposits on the road remind us that horse transport was very much the norm in the early 1900s.

High Street W. Glossop

23 & 24. Two postcards reproduced on this and the page opposite were date stamped August 30th 1905. The trams by now had become a familiar sight, although the interest shown in the cameraman suggests perhaps that photography was still something which attracted curiosity. The building lines are again identifiable, even allowing for such things as superficial alterations of shop

fronts, advertising hoardings, etc. In both views, the Victoria Inn – latterly renamed 'Corner Cupboard' – helps to locate Arundel Street, the point which Car No.5 is passing on its way to Hadfield.

Posters to the right give notice of the Centenary celebrations by the Wesleyan Church, whilst the Great Central Railway was offering excursions to Blackpool. *Photos: courtesy A.K. Kirby*

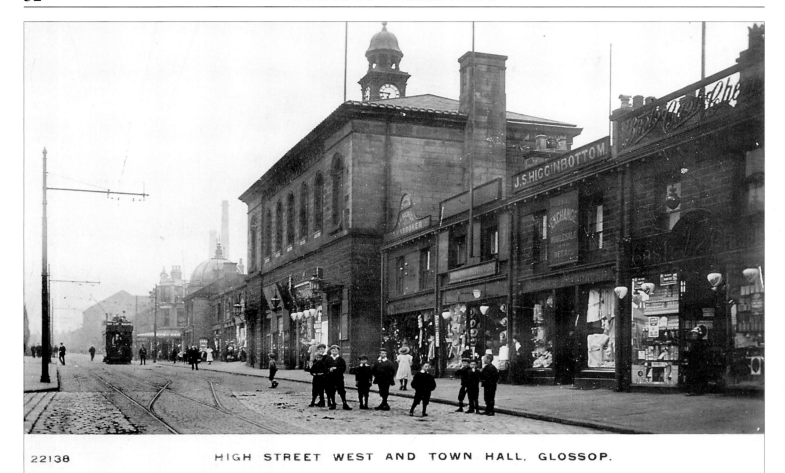

22138   HIGH STREET WEST AND TOWN HALL, GLOSSOP.

25. This view along High Street West is not dated but plainly illustrates how little Glossop town centre changed during the 'tram' era. The postcard from which the view is taken was produced for Boots Cash Chemists, whose shop is to the right of the picture. The card carried a message from a Mrs Jessie Massey, of Ashby, Doncaster, who had addressed it Hawkshead, Glossop.

Photo: Pelham, Sheffield, courtesy A.K. Kirby.

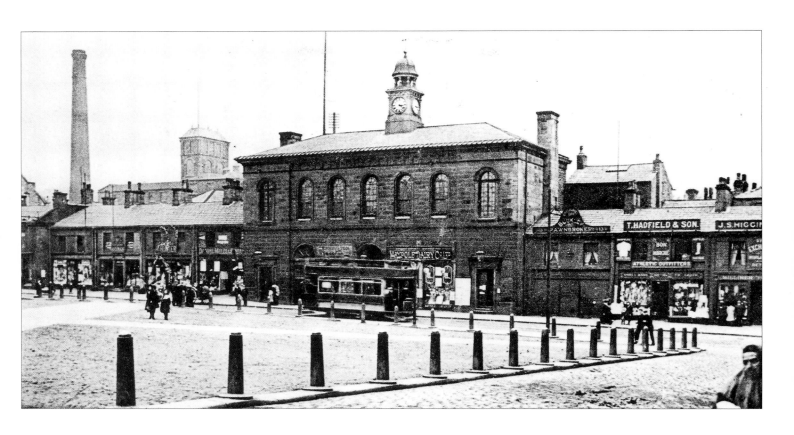

26. Norfolk Square and the Town Hall, with a service car waiting on the turnout for trade to Old Glossop. The tall chimney and upperworks of Howard Town Mills loom up on the left.

27. Both this view of Norfolk Square – and that on page 32, illustrate that both bus and tram were operating alongside each other for a short time. Although dated July 1928, the tram service had been withdrawn so one assumes the photograph to have been taken perhaps in 1927. The bus, one of the early North Western types, has a MOTTRAM destination board located to the right above the radiator grille. The *Glossop Dale New Industrial & Co-operative Society Ltd* obviously have some occasion to celebrate with bunting and banners proclaiming some important event

Photo: courtesy A.K. Kirby

28. This scene looks west along the Square, picking out the east end of the 350 foot long loop. The connecting lines south to the Whitfield spur curve left just in front of the carthorse. Figures pose in statuesque array, including a vigilant inspector.

29. Glossop Tramway tickets from the collection of W.H. Bett, printed by Williamsons of Ashton, and deriving from the post World War 1 era. The 1d Child ticket is mauve, the 2d blue, the 3d yellow and the 4d white.

30. A careful inspection will reveal no less than three tramcars in this 1903 shot of the Square, including one on the left heading for Charlestown down Victoria Street. A heavily loaded woodcart provides a point of interest. At this time the dome was known as 'Bradbury's Corner' and housed a shaving saloon. A little earlier it was the premises of Rossons Chemists.

31. Although the chimneys of the Howard Town Mills continue to emit smoke. the town seems to be in the midst of a quiet spell, confirmed in some respects by the notice in Hepworth's window which indicates that the shop is, or will be, closed during Wakes Holidays. The postcard is date stamped 1923 and the double juction for the Whitfield 'spur' is well illustrated here on its turn into Victoria Street. One person obviously at work however is the street sweep, seen to the right of the lady in the long dress, clearing the animal droppings to one side of High Street East. Norfolk Street is immediately to the left. *Photo: courtesy A.K. Kirby*

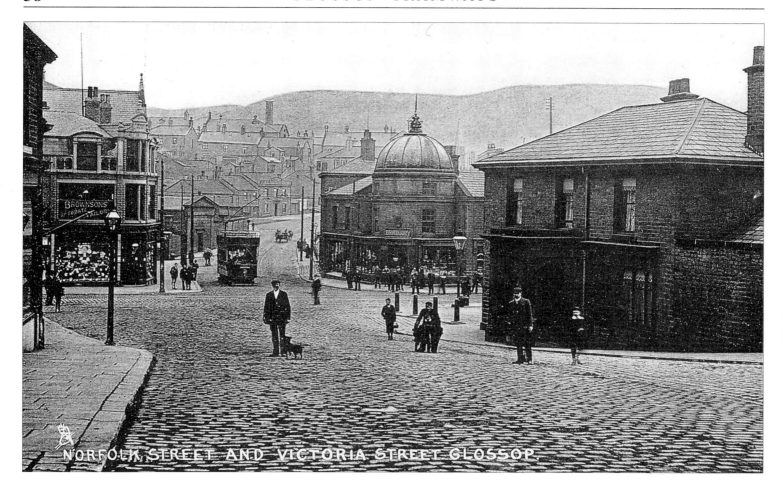

NORFOLK STREET AND VICTORIA STREET GLOSSOP.

32. A final view of the locality looking south down Norfolk Street, revealing a sea of cobbles, posing pedestrians, and Car 1 taking the Whitfield line. The background to this photograph has been extensively retouched.

33. The eastern end of High Street East again reveals rows of well-built terraces along the line of the tramway. In the distance the Commercial Hotel can just be glimpsed as the tramtracks swing hard left on to Hall Street and the final stretch of the main line. Four proud ladies display bouncing babies for the camera. Are any still alive today, one wonders?

34. The junction of High Street East and Hall Street (renamed Manor Park Road in 1926) had a loop laid on the bend, which Car 6 is just entering. The Commercial Hotel is on the right, and on the left is a fine water trough with some splendid ornamental ironwork supporting a street lamp. A feeder box stands alongside the nearest bracket pole.

35. A view taken just after the start of tram services shows children happily playing at the junction of Hall Street and High Street East. It is just possible to see the sign belonging to the 'Commercial Hotel' in the top right hand of the picture. The two and a half minutes that it took for the tram to travel into the town would now no doubt be appreciated, particularly with a fare of threepence (2p).

During the week, trams to Glossop and Hadfield called here on no less than 56 occasions with extra on Fridays and Saturdays. Those travelling *to* Old Glossop enjoyed a marginally better service, with trams calling 59 times.

Photo: courtesy A.K. Kirby

36. The Old Glossop terminus, showing two of the three public houses nearby, the Talbot Inn with the Hare and Hounds beyond. The line terminated in a loop, with a short length of single line beyond, stretching in front of the horse's hoofs.

37. An interesting close-up from a Victoria Street scene showing a pre-World War 1 Whitfield Church Walk, but revealing other interesting details. The little demi-car is caught among the worshippers in their Sunday best, and immediately behind it an open-top tram moves along High Street with two ladies occupying the upper deck front seats. The nearest tram standard carries a variant style of stop sign.

38. A view taken from the same direction but further south, showing a car heading towards Norfolk Square. Note how far across the offset trolley arm has swung to remain on the running wire. The rustic building on the left is the theatre, and Collier Street leads off to the right. Offloaded passengers head home across a vast expanse of cobblestones.

39. Taken at the highest point of Victoria Road just above Derby Street, this postcard view looks towards town with the tower of the former Littlemoor School and Chapel on the right. Note the 'STOP' sign painted on the nearest standard, and the milk cart in the middle distance. One car went out of control down this slope in 1904 and ended up on the High Street pavement.

40. A decorated tramcar pictured in Norfolk Square. Although the date and occasion are unknown, the bells, portraits and garlands suggest it celebrated a wedding, perhaps involving one of the tramway staff.

41. A superb study of the demi-car at the Charlestown Road terminus loop, outside the gates of Whitfield House (now the entrance to Glossop Fire Station). Standing alongside is motorman John Byrom in appropriate heavy duty footwear. The photograph captures the major features of the small tramcar to perfection.

List of Publications

Scenes from the Past series

1. Railways around Stockport
2. Railways around Buxton
3. Manchester Railway Termini
4. Cambrian Coast Railway
5. Railways around Grimsby, Cleethorpes, Immingham and North East Lincolnshire
6. Railways around Preston: an historical view
7. Railway from Buxton to Bakewell, Matlock and Ambergate
8. Railways in and around the Manchester Suburbs
9 The Llangollen Line – Ruabon to Barmouth
10. Railways in and around Bolton
11. Railways in and around Nottingham
12. The Railways of North Wales – The Conwy Valley Line Blaenau Ffestiniog to Llandudno Junction

For details of price and availability ask your bookseller or send s.a.e. to:

Foxline
Publishing

32 Urwick Road
Romiley
STOCKPORT SK6 3JS
Telephone: 061 430 6834

Tramways – and other historic 'ways' **in and around Stockport**

☆ For over fifty years, the tram car provided transport for the masses in and around Stockport. This book takes the reader on nostalgic journeys through the districts surrounding the town – Hazel Grove, Cheadle, Bredbury, Woodley, Hyde etc – together with one of the author's 'favourite ways', a trip to Manchester.
☆ Raymond Keeley gives his individualistic approach to the subject by including the occasional view of his other great interest – railways, at a time when integrated transport was taken for granted.

80pp., 160 + illustrations £6.95. 27,000 words of text and captions.

ISBN 1-870119-09-6   Card cover.

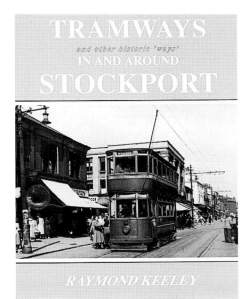